W9-CIR-650

Jean-Paul Ameline
curator

Guide to
the permanent collection

Musée national
d'art moderne

© éditions du Centre Pompidou,
éditions Scala
Paris 1986
© ADAGP Paris 1986
© SPADEM Paris 1986

The Musée national d'art moderne is one of the four departments of the Georges Pompidou Centre, the other three being the Bibliothèque publique d'information (B P I), the Centre de création industrielle (C C I) and the Institut de recherche et coordination acoustique/musique (I R C A M). However, the Museum is the only one of these departments whose existence predates the Centre itself.

The Museum was founded in **1947**, *mainly due to the efforts of Jean Cassou, its first curator, and of Georges Salles, director of the Musées de France, towards giving Modern Art its rightful place in the national heritage.*

1947 to 1977 *the collections formerly housed at the Luxemburg museum (living artists) and Jeu de Paume museum (foreign schools) were united at the Palais de Tokyo in the Avenue du Président Wilson in Paris. These collections were subsequently enriched by a comprehensive policy of acquisition of 20th century works, both by purchase and by donation.*

1967 *saw the creation of the Centre national d'art contemporain (C N A C) with a view to grouping together documentation, purchases and commissions to artists under a single authority. The advent of the C N A C also marked the beginning of a new French international policy in regard to both the exhibition and acquisition of Modern Art.*

1977 *the Museum was moved to the Pompidou Centre and given its own purchasing budget. This allowed the museum to enrich its reserves considerably. Today the Museum possesses over 15 000 works which together form one of the most important collections of Modern Art in the world.*

map
index

4

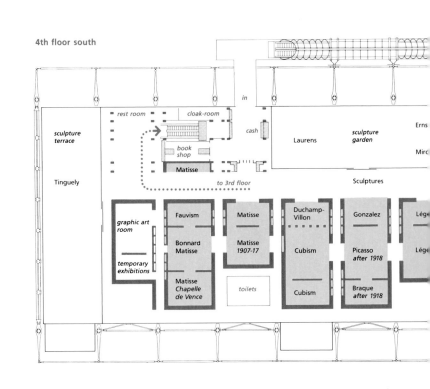

4th floor south

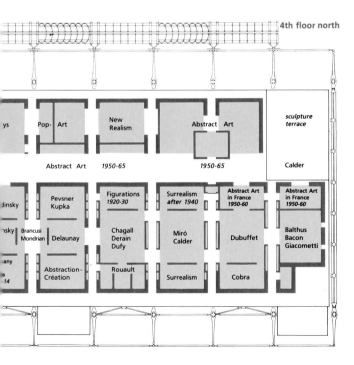

4th floor north

ys | Pop- Art | New Realism | Abstract Art | sculpture terrace

Abstract Art | 1950-65 | 1950-65 | Calder

dinsky | Pevsner Kupka | Figurations 1920-30 | Surrealism after 1940 | Abstract Art in France 1950-60 | Abstract Art in France 1950-60

nsky | Brancusi Mondrian | Delaunay | Chagall Derain Dufy | Miró Calder | Dubuffet | Balthus Bacon Giacometti

any | Abstraction- Création | Rouault | Surrealism | Cobra

6

3rd floor south

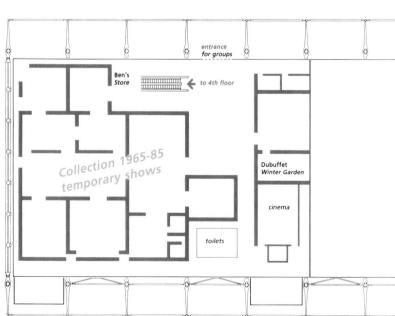

entrance
for groups

Ben's
Store

to 4th floor

Collection 1965-85
temporary shows

Dubuffet
Winter Garden

cinema

toilets

4th floor
south

MATISSE BONNARD FAUVISM

1888-89 Foundation of the *Nabi* group in Paris including Pierre Bonnard, Maurice Denis, Aristide Maillol, Paul Sérusier, Edouard Vuillard, etc.

1905 The critic Louis Vauxcelles uses the word *"fauve"* ("wild beast"), to describe certain paintings by Derain, Marquet, Matisse, Rouault, Van Dongen, Vlaminck, etc. exhibited together at the Salon d'Automne of Paris.

1906 Matisse's first visit to Northern Africa. At the same time, Matisse develops an interest in Islamic and African art.

1921 From now on, Matisse spends his time in Nice and Paris.

1925 Bonnard takes up residence in the South of France.

1943-51 Matisse works on large *"gouaches découpées"* (paper cut-outs) especially for designs and decorations of the Chapel of the Rosary, Vence.

4th floor south

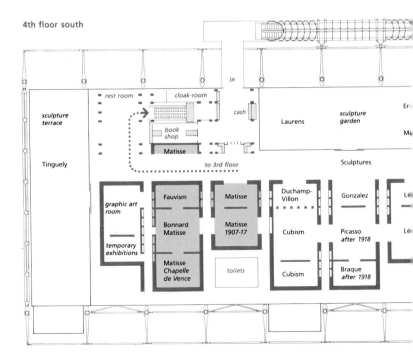

Sorrow of the King
1952

"When the means are so
refined and reduced that their
expressive power is exhausted,
we must return to the essential
principles which originally
formed the language of mankind. Thus it is the principles
which are on the way
back up, which are growing
stronger, that give us new life.
Paintings represent refinement,
subtle erosion, inert blends:
They use beautiful blues,
beautiful reds, beautiful
yellows, the kinds of things
that stir men's fundamental
sensuality. This is the starting
point of Fauvism, which entails
having the courage to seek
purer means."

Henri Matisse
Interview with E. Teriade
Minotaure n° 9
October 1936

In his last years (1951-54) Matisse devoted
himself to the technique of gouache cutouts.
He had first used them to complete a mural
composition in the USA (*La Danse* 1932) and
subsequently in his *Jazz* illustrations (1947).
Matisse found that the novel method of
the cutout enabled him to resolve the conflict
between line and colour; by using scissors,
he could combine every aspect of his work
—painting, drawing, and sculpture—in a single
creation. Here, two musicians and a dancing girl
(suggested by her white veils and her toes) are
positioned against a background of coloured
rectangles. Flying golden sparks call to mind both
the movements of the girl and the peals of music
to which she is dancing.

Henri Matisse
La Tristesse du Roi
Sorrow of the King
1952
cut and pasted paper
prepainted with gouache 292 × 386

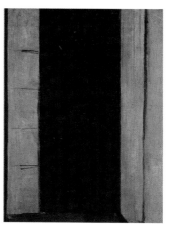

1 Arabesque: ornamental curved line around objects, constituting an essential rhythmic element within a painted composition.

Matisse first achieved fame as a leader of the *Fauvist movement*; but after 1907, he developed a form of painting, influenced by Gauguin, Cézanne and African Decorative Art, which disclaimed the traditional laws of representational art. By the use of flat tints, arabesques[1] and a frontal approach to subjects, Matisse's art gradually became a universe of *"forms reduced to essential,"* with the aim of giving the onlooker *"the purest intellectual pleasure and repose"* (Henri Matisse) through their balance and sensuality.

Matisse's work between 1908 and 1954, was continually developed and deepened; after flirting with Cubism and Abstract Art (*Porte-Fenêtre à Collioure* 1914), Matisse emerged in 1920 with a more decorative conception of painting in which colour was freed from its subservience to line and of any purely descriptive function. In this way, the full expressive power of colour could be brought into play. (*Figure décorative sur fond ornemental* 1925).

After 1930, Matisse experimented in the USA and in France with large mural compositions; among the most ambitious of these is the decoration of the Chapelle de Vence (1948-51). At the same time, his work as a sculptor (*Nus de dos* 1909-30) and illustrator are classic references in 20th century Art.

Henri Matisse
Figure décorative sur fond ornemental
Decorative figure on an ornamental ground
1925-26
oil on canvas 130 × 98

Henri Matisse
Porte-fenêtre à Collioure
The open window, Collioure
1914
oil on canvas 116 × 89

Le Luxe I
1907

11

This great painting represents a decisive simplification of Matisse's art. Three crudely outlined monumental figures are placed in a landscape that is merely suggested by contrasting hot and cold colours.

The brushwork is tense and thin, covering the surface with flat tints and elementary, deliberately unfinished forms.

The painting's title echoes that of an earlier work, with Baudelairean overtones, from Matisse's *"pointilliste"* period: *"Luxe, calme et volupté"* (1905 - Paris, Musée d'Orsay). Nonetheless, contrasting as it does with the generally austere nature of the painting, this title shares in the latent mysteriousness which is characteristic of so many of Matisse's works.

Henri Matisse
Le Luxe I
1907
oil on canvas 210 × 138

Henri Matisse
Nu de dos, premier état
Back I
1909
bronze 190 × 116 × 13

Henri Matisse
Nu de dos, quatrième état
Back IV
1930
bronze 190 × 114 × 16

Here, the oblique lines of the bay windows in the artist's studio divide two different worlds. On the outside, painted in cold colours, are the garden and the mosaic of roofs on the hillside above Cannes. On the inside are the warm, intimate shadows of the *atelier*, blended with the shapes of familiar objects, and the outline of a face.

And yet, there is no opposition whatever between the two parts of this painting; borne by tightly-interlacing colour tones, the eye roves freely across a calm surface. Every corner of the canvas seems to be suffused by dazzling light—and this light seems to flow from the great yellow mimosa tree outside the windows.

Pierre Bonnard's formative years were influenced by the *Nabis* group (Sérusier, Roussel, Vuillard, Maillol) for whom a painting was "*essentially a flat surface covered in colours which have been assembled in a certain order*" (Maurice Denis). He became well known around 1900 for his posters, book illustrations, and painted panels, which reflected the decorative style of Japanese prints in somewhat unexpected arrangements.

Bonnard knew Monet between 1910 and 1916, and subsequently (1925) went to live on the Côte d'Azur. These two milestones in his career set him on a course that continued until his death: by "*interpreting light, form and features with colour only*", Bonnard discovered a pictorial method by which objects, dissolving into feathery brushwork, seem to recede and vanish into a general harmony of intense colour.

The work of Bonnard was for many years considered as an impressionist intrusion into the 20th century. It has now been rediscovered because of the specifically pictorial experience it represents (subjectivity, representation, the role of colour).

Pierre Bonnard
Portrait de l'artiste dans la glace du cabinet de toilette
Self-portrait in the bathroom mirror
1939-45
oil on canvas 73 × 51

Pierre Bonnard
L'atelier au mimosa
The studio and mimosa
1939-46
oil on canvas 127 × 127

13

In 1905, at the Salon d'Automne in Paris, the art critic Louis Vauxcelles described the paintings of Derain, Marquet, Matisse, Vlaminck, etc., which were being exhibited together, as the work of *"fauves"* ("wild beasts") because of their violent colours.

The Fauvists, as they quickly came to be known, sought to follow the example of Gauguin, Van Gogh and Signac in substituting emotive power for the "illusory" imitation of nature, by the use of *"intensely coloured equivalents"* (Matisse) of light and space. From 1900 onwards, they began to reject the conventional laws of light and shade, the reproduction of relief and localised tones[1] to achieve tonal purity, and the contrast of colour and touch as a means to summarize forms.

In 1906, Braque, Dufy and Friesz joined the Fauvists and in Germany the *Die Brücke*[2] "expressionist" group established relations with them. But, after 1907, the movement disintegrated, Matisse, Derain and Braque (for example) being more concerned with rigour and construction. From this time onwards, each followed his own road.

[1] Localised tone: the tone of an object seen in the light of day, independant of surrounding shades or accidental light.

[2] See *Avant-gardes in Europe* Germany, Italy, Russia. page 29

Georges Braque
L'Estaque
1906
oil on canvas 50 × 60

André Derain
Les deux péniches
Two coal barges
1906
oil on canvas 80 × 97

Raoul Dufy
Les affiches à Trouville
Posters at Trouville
1906
oil on canvas 65 × 81

C U B I S M

September **1907**	Picasso paints *Les Demoiselles d'Avignon* (New York, Museum of Modern Art) in which the basic theories of Cubism are laid down for the first time.
November **1907**	Cézanne retrospective in Paris.
November **1908**	First Braque exhibition at the Kahnweiler Gallery in Paris. The art critic Louis Vauxcelles makes the remark that *"... he reduces everything [...] to cubes"* and the movement is baptised "Cubism".
March and November **1911**	Léger, Delaunay, Gleizes and Metzinger jointly exhibit their "cubist" work at the Salon des Indépendants and the Salon d'Automne.
May to September **1912**	Picasso and Braque create their first *collages* and *papiers collés*.
October **1912**	Apogee of the Cubist movement at the *Section d'Or* exhibition in Paris (works by Delaunay, Duchamp, Duchamp-Villon, Gleizes, Gris, La Fresnaye, Léger, Metzinger, Picabia, Villon).
1914-19	Gradual dissolution of the Cubist movement.

4th floor south

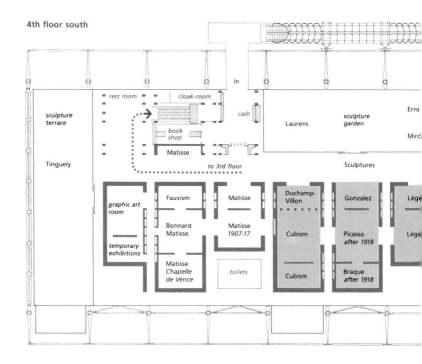

The Great Horse   *Bottle and glass*
1914-66   *1917*

Out of a leaping horse, Duchamp-Villon has fashioned a symbol of pure energy, combining organic vigour and mechanical power. The limbs of this creature have become gears; its head, mane and neck swell out to extend the body's forward thrust, which is expressed by a set of connecting rods that link the front of the structure to the rear, seeming to reveal all the hidden machinery of effort. This sculpture was completed on a small scale in 1914, fifty years after the artist's death, several much larger casts were made of it by his brothers, Jacques Villon and Marcel Duchamp.

15

This construction by the sculptor Laurens, a friend of Braque after 1911, is Cubist from many different stand-points. It is thoroughly Cubist, firstly, in terms of its junk materials (sheet metal, plywood, wood); secondly, in terms of the various insights it offers (cork of the bottle evoked from above by a round piece of wood; hollowed-out profile as seen from within; level of liquid shown on a slant); and thirdly, in terms of the colour-plane distribution around the cylinder, which dynamically suggests the presence of surrounding space.

Raymond Duchamp-Villon
Le cheval majeur
The Great Horse
1914-66
bronze
cast in 1976 150 × 97 × 153

Henri Laurens
Bouteille et verre
Bottle and glass
1917
polychromed wood and sheet metal
67 × 27 × 24

The Cubist revolution of 1907-19 was produced by the shock waves sent through the artistic and literary milieux of Paris by the discoveries of Picasso and Braque. These discoveries were attuned to the concerns of the post-Cézanne artistic generation, and they constituted the most radical upheaval in early 20th century art.

By painting things "*as one thinks them, not as one sees them*" (Picasso), Cubism placed conception over imitation in the representing of reality. Thus the work of art became "*a pictorial fact*" (Braque), or "*an organism which carries its raison d'être within itself*" (Gleizes).

Modern sculpture was also radically transformed by Cubism (Duchamp-Villon, Laurens, Lipchitz). While experimenting with colours and new materials, sculpture also abandoned appearances based on vision and replaced them with an architectural reconstruction of the rhythm of forms (structuration by planes, spatial integration).

Juan Gris
Le petit déjeuner
The breakfast table
1915
oil and charcoal on canvas 92 × 73

Francis Picabia
Udnie
1913
oil on canvas 290 × 300

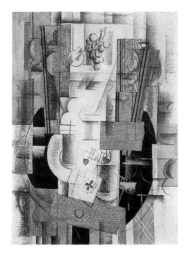

Between 1907 and 1914, Picasso and Braque broke with the perspective system of the Renaissance, by introducing a new way of representing forms in relation to space. In doing this, they were influenced by Cézanne's reconstruction of volume by interwoven planes of colour and by the geometric representation of the human figure in Primitive Art. Little by little, after 1907, the consensus that there was only one way in which objects could be observed (a point of view stemming from the laws of linear perspective), was abandoned. Picasso began to break objects into fragments with facets corresponding to different axes of vision (Picasso *Femme assise* 1910). Braque placed them in spaces which had themselves been *"materialised"* into monochrome camaieu[1] of angular planes; these replaced the play of light and shade in conventional painting. This *"absolute possession of things"* (Braque) paradoxically resulted around 1910 in a formal explosion, with allusive "signs" (flattened letters, musical notes, trompe-l'œil, nails, etc.) being included in the painting to make it easier to decode. After 1912, the essential attributes of objects were preserved, in order to make the composition easier to understand and more decorative (Braque *Compotier et cartes* 1913). This development marked the transition, according to the accepted terms, from *"Analytical"* to *"Synthetic"* Cubism.

[1] Camaieu: monochrome painting, whose play of colour tones (light to dark) gives the impression of a relief.

Georges Braque
Compotier et cartes
Still life with fruit dish and cards
1913
oil, gouache and charcoal on canvas 80 × 59

Pablo Picasso
Etude d'une des "Demoiselles d'Avignon"
Study for "Les Demoiselles d'Avignon"
1907
oil on canvas 66 × 59

Seated Woman
1910

The image is the mind's pure
creation. It is born not of the
comparison, but of the relation
between two more or less
different and distant realities.
The more different these two
realities are and the more apt
their relationship, the stronger
the image will be and the
deeper its fund of emotive
power and poetic reality.
It serves no useful purpose to
bring together two realities
which intrinsically have nothing
to do with one another, for no
image can be created as a
result. They are simply opposed.
It is rare that this kind of
opposition engenders power.
An image is not powerful
because it is brutal or fantastic,
but because the ideas it
contains each come from afar,
and their association is apt.
The result immediately
demonstrates the aptness
of the association (...)

Pierre Reverdy
L'Image
from Nord-Sud, n° 13
March 1918

Out of a monochrome background of
greys and browns looms a seated human figure,
only recognisable as such by her oval face
and rounded shoulders.

On the other hand, a highly complex
combination of light and dark facets suggests the
volumes of the head and torso, and reveals both
the source of the light and the actual position of
the body on the chair (the right side is brought
forward and highlighted, and the left side recedes
into a darker background). The plastic energy
emanating from the woman's writhing chest gives
her a flayed-alive look; she seems to conform
to her formal tempo, rather than the codified
laws of anatomy.

Pablo Picasso
Femme assise
Seated Woman
1910
oil on canvas 100 × 73

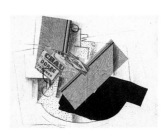

When, in May 1912, Picasso placed a piece
of oilcloth in his *Nature morte à la chaise
cannée* (Paris, Musée Picasso) to imitate the
caning of a chair, he was the first artist to use
collage, or the application to a canvas of
material other than paint. A few months later,
Braque made his first *papier collé* by directly
attaching a piece of paper, painted to imitate
wood, to a charcoal drawing: the *papier collé*
was intended to represent a table on which
objects had been placed.

By the use of these new methods, reality
could be either suggested by a play of
figurative analogies, (often humorous) or
merely positioned on the canvas just as it was,
instead of being represented. At the same
time, because of their intrinsic qualities and
colours, the new materials could achieve
perspective, hence depth; the artist using
them could escape the cubist monochrome
without recourse to paint. In short, the
novelty of improvised *papiers collés, collages*
and *assemblages* superseded both the traditional opposition of painting and sculpture,
and the habitual methods of representation
taught by art history.

Pablo Picasso
Tête d'homme au chapeau
Man's head with hat
1912-13
charcoal, pasted paper
and sand, mounted on paper 65 × 49

Georges Braque
Compotier et cartes
Still life with fruit dish and cards
1913
oil, gouache and charcoal on canvas
80 × 59

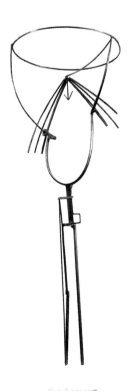

The sculptor Julio Gonzalez came from a family of Barcelona silversmiths. He was trained as a welder at the Renault car factory and began to sculpt in metal around 1927, creating masks, figurines and still lives with pieces of sheet iron.

In 1928, his meeting with Picasso proved decisive; the metal constructions which Picasso undertook with his technical assistance encouraged Gonzalez to go a step further. In 1930-31, he began to use the principle of steel rod assemblage to integrate space in his sculptures. His goal in this was to *"project and delineate things within space, using new methods; to take advantage of that space and build with it, as if it were a newly-obtained material."*

Gonzalez had links with the Surrealists, as well as with the first abstract movements. Between 1930 and 1937, he produced works in which his virtuosity enabled him to juxtapose abstract art and naturalist evocations.

Julio Gonzalez
Femme à la corbeille
Woman with basket
c. 1930-33
iron 194 × 63 × 63

Julio Gonzalez
Petite danseuse
Little dancer
1934-37
iron 17,5 × 10 × 4

Figure
c. 1927

"To my great misfortune, and maybe also to my joy, I tend to put things in my paintings according to my current love affairs. How sad to be a painter who likes blondes, but forbids himself to put them in his pictures because they don't go with baskets of fruit!" (...)

"For me, a finished painting is the end of a series of destructions. I paint a picture, then I destroy it. But in the end nothing is lost—because the red I took away from one place reappears somewhere else." (...)

"I treat paintings just as I treat things. I do a window in just the same way as I would look through one. If an open window doesn't look right in the painting, I draw the curtain and close it just like I would in my bedroom. In painting, as in life, you have to take direct action." (...)

Christian Zervos
Conversation avec Picasso
in Cahiers d'Art
n°[s] 7-10, 1935

Four locks of hair like drumsticks, a nose like a pig's snout, a gash of a mouth pointing vertically upward, two crudely stylized, wide-apart, empty eyes; the work of a surrealist-influenced Picasso, who is giving free rein to his iconoclastic fantasies. But this nightmarish profile, more "biomorphic" than human, is also a sculptural assemblage: though the painting has neither relief nor colour, it is completely imprisoned within an emphatic black line which could just as well be a length of steel wire. This painting opened up a new avenue for Picasso, which he explored after 1928 with the sculptor Julio Gonzalez: open-form sculpture in metal.

1917-25
"Curvilinear" Cubism
and "classical" representation

1925-31
Surrealist influence

1931-34
Concentration on sculpture
at Boisgeloup (Eure)

1934-39
Tensions in private life.
Spanish Civil War: Picasso paints
Guernica (Madrid, Prado)

1939-44
Stays in Paris during the Occupation

1944-73
Living on the Côte d'Azur.
Sculpture, ceramics,
then a return to painting via
Delacroix, Velasquez, Manet, David.
Monumental portraits

Pablo Picasso
Femme en gris dite *« La Liseuse »*
Woman in grey "Woman reading"
1920
oil on canvas 166 × 102

Pablo Picasso
L'Aubade
1942
oil on canvas 195 × 265

"Braque, like Van Gogh and Vermeer,
unquestionably had a special secret of his own.
His work is always mysteriously full and satisfying;
fluid but never airless; radiant, yet without the
least source of light; dramatic, without
the smallest pretext; tranquil, yet alert; and
so carefully considered as to give the impression of
a mirage superimposed on reality.

But as soon as I try to put a name to the secret
of Braque, or to what I feel about him, I arrive at
this: tirelessly, Braque makes of lemons, grilled
fish and tablecloths what they were waiting to be,
indeed what they always yearned to become; their
own family ghosts."

Jean Paulhan
Braque le Patron
Geneva-Paris
1948

Georges Braque
L'Oiseau et son nid
Bird and its nest
1955
oil and sand on canvas 130 × 173

Georges Braque
Fruits sur une nappe et compotier
Fruit on a tablecloth with fruit dish
1925
oil on canvas 130 × 75

Fernand Léger

1881-1955

Fernand Léger was associated with the Cubist movement between 1909 and 1914. He based his early research on what he called the *"law of contrasts"*. By opposing flat, coloured surfaces to volumes modelled in grey relief like curved or angular fragments, he created powerful rhythms within forms linked to one another which eventually ceased to bear any resemblance to representational art (*Contraste de formes* 1913).

During the First World War, during which he was *"dazzled by the breech of a 75 cannon standing open in the sunshine"*, Léger moved closer to the representation of modern life; machines, landscapes disrupted by posters and pylons, human beings totally devoid of sentimentality (*La lecture* 1924). Geometrical figures and objects appeared in his canvasses contrasted with forms, reliefs and colours. After 1920, Léger's meeting with the architects Le Corbusier and Mallet-Stevens led to an interest in monumental painting, integrated with architecture; at the time, this had a completely new social significance. With his divers, acrobats and cyclists, organised into gigantic shapes and confronted by immensities of flat colour, Léger found what he was looking for: *"the greatest possible degree of dynamism: free colour and free form."*

Fernand Léger
Contraste de formes
Contrast of forms
1913
oil on canvas 100 × 81

Fernand Léger
La lecture
Reading
1924
oil on canvas 113 × 146

4th floor
north

ABSTRACT ART 1910-35

Munich **1910** Kandinsky's first abstract aquarelle.

Paris **1912** Kupka shows two non-figurative paintings at the Salon d'Automne.

Paris **1912-13** Delaunay's *Fenêtres* (Windows) and *Formes circulaires* (Circular forms).

Russia **1913** Malevitch's *Carré noir sur fond blanc* (Black square).

Holland **1913-14** Mondrian's first abstract composition.

Switzerland **1915** Hans Arp's first abstract *papiers collés*.

Florence **1915** Magnelli's first abstract paintings.

Germany **1919** Founding of the *Bauhaus* at Weimar (with Kandinsky, Klee, Moholy-Nagy, etc.).

Russia **1920-27** Constructivist Movement (Gabo, El Lissitsky, Pevsner, Rodchenko, Tatlin, etc.).

Paris **1931** Foundation of the *Abstraction-Création* group; 400 artists of all nations (including Arp, Delaunay, Gabo, Herbin, Kupka, Sophie Taeuber-Arp, van Doesburg, Vantongerloo).

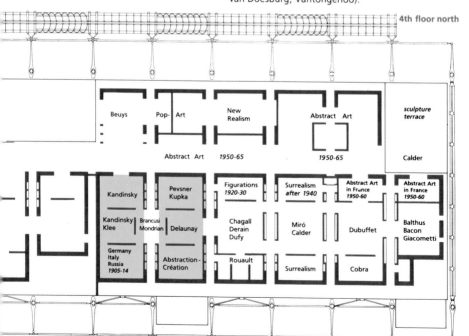

Kandinsky may have owed his taste for the expressive power of colours and the evocative power of music to his Russian origins. At all events, in Munich between 1908 and 1911, he was the first to take the decisive step towards Abstract Art, with his fiery interpretation of the emotion inspired in him by the landscapes of Upper Bavaria. As time went by, Kandinsky's paintings became more and more divorced from any reference to reality.

Between 1911 and 1914, Kandinsky produced a succession of *Impressions, Improvisations* and *Compositions* (titles chosen for their musical connotation). As he saw it, the power of conveying the world's mystery by *"exact vibration"* belonged to forms viewed as *"spiritual beings"* and to colours endowed with true *"inner sonority."*

After a five-year stay in Russia (1917-22) Kandinsky returned to Germany as a professor at the Bauhaus (1922-33) and developed a *"grammar of forms"* to which colour gave a quality of inner palpitation.

During his exile in Paris (1933-44) after the closure of the Bauhaus by the Nazis, he contrived in his last paintings to reconcile reality and the abstract under the banner of *"Concrete Art"*. This was done by the use of scintillating forms and zoomorphic figures outlined with meticulous care. Kandinsky *"conjured up original, imperishable forces and obliged them to flow into his paintings and his poetry. These forces have dissolved the unreal foundations of reality in his work, so that a slight vibration is all that remains of the palpable world"* (Jean Arp).

Vassily Kandinsky
Sur blanc II
On white II
1923
oil on canvas 105 × 98

Vassily Kandinsky
sans titre
Untitled water-colour
1910
pencil, water-colour
and india ink on paper 49 × 64

28

As a result of donations made
in 1966 and 1978, and
to the bequest of Mme Nina
Kandinsky (1980), the Museum
has become one of the world's
most important repositories of
Kandinsky's work.

*"All roads lead to the eye, to a point where images
meet and acquire form. From this process comes a
synthesis between exterior observation and inner
vision. It is here, at this point of juncture, that hand-
created forms take root and spring up; though they
may be completely unlike the physical aspect of the
object observed, nonetheless, from the standpoint of
Totality, they are not at variance with it."*

Paul Klee
1923
from *Théorie de l'Art Moderne*
P.H. Gonthier
Geneva 1968

Paul Klee
Rythmisches
Rythmical
1930
oil on canvas 69 × 50

Vassily Kandinsky
Avec l'arc noir
With the black arch
1912
oil on canvas 188 × 198

The European avant-garde between 1905-1914 gave painting a revolutionary mission within the broad framework of a project to free the creative power of Humanity from the servitudes and conventions of bourgeois society. The painter's art, in short, was to express both the emotional intensity of experience and the swirling dynamism of the world. This determination to completely regenerate art rested on the examples of Gauguin and Van Gogh, but also on the discovery of the stunning expressive power of Primitive and Popular Art, and the aesthetic progress made by Fauvism and Cubism. All this explains the creative effervescence which convulsed the art worlds of Germany, Italy and Russia on the eve of the First World War. Thus, while the German "Expressionists" of the *Die Brücke*[1] group (Kirchner, Schmidt-Rottluff, Heckel, Nolde, Pechstein) were translating their violent feelings by exaggerating plastic dissonances, it was, on the contrary, the "spiritual" harmony of forms and colours which was sought by the members of the *Blaue Reiter*[2] of Munich (Jawlensky, Kandinsky, Klee, Franz Marc, etc.). In another development, the representation of the simultaneity of visual sensations in modern life was the objective of the Italian *Futurists*[3] (Balla, Boccioni, Severini) and the Russian *Cubo-Futurists* (Gontcharova, Larionov, Pougny). Through the fragmentation of space and the blending of figures and backgrounds, they contrived to make their works into networks of "dynamic lines of force", which came close to Abstract Art.

[1] *The Bridge* founded 1905 in Dresden, dissolved 1913 in Berlin.

[2] *The Blue Rider* (1911-13).

[3] The first *Futurist Manifesto* was published in Paris, 1909, by Italian writer Marinetti.

Michel Larionov
Promenade, Vénus de boulevard
c. 1912-13
oil on canvas 116 × 86

Ernst-Ludwig Kirchner
Toilette (Frau vor dem Spiegel)
Dressing (Woman in front of a mirror)
1913-20
oil on canvas 100 × 75

Alberto Magnelli
Explosion lyrique n° 8, Florence 1918
Lyric explosion number 8, Florence 1918
1918
oil on canvas 101 × 76

1876-1957

Brancusi came to Paris in 1904. His parents were Rumanian peasants and Brancusi himself was completely self-educated, with a prodigious gift as a jack-of-all-trades.

Beginning in 1908, he set out to banish detail from his sculptures, paring them down to their essential volumes: oval, cylindrical or cubic. The surfaces were either polished to perfection or left rough, this procedure allowed the material to express its own intrinsic qualities. Brancusi believed that *"it is not the exterior form of things which is real, but their essence."* Thus by 1920, he had arrived at abstraction by the purification of forms as a means of expressing the forces of nature. His sculptures were divested of *"the last vestiges of reality"* and became more and more monumental, as with the *Endless Column*, 30 metres high, which he erected at Tirgu-Jiu, Rumania, in 1937.

Though he became the darling of the entire international avant-garde, Brancusi clung to the simplicity of a reclusive artist until the end of his life. He lived in Montparnasse in a studio which he had converted with his own hands, and which he left, untouched, to the French state in 1956.

Brancusi's studio now stands in front of the Centre Georges Pompidou, on the piazza Beaubourg
(See page 70 conditions of visit).

Constantin Brancusi
Le Coq
The Cock
1935
polished bronze 103 × 21 × 11
base of wood and stone 151 × 47 × 39

Constantin Brancusi
La Muse endormie
Sleeping Muse
1910
polished bronze 16 × 18,5 × 27

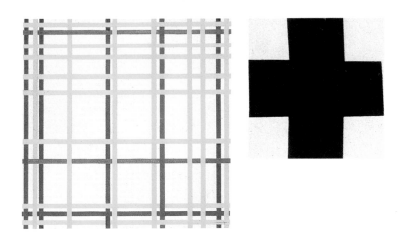

Abstract Art, which began with
the investigations and experiments of
Impressionism, Symbolism and Cubism, was
primarily the result of radical new thinking on
the ability of modern painting to free Colour
and Form of the contradictions inherent in
the representation of the objective world.
Consequently, colours and forms became, in
themselves, the ultimate means available
to define *"the purest representation of
Universality"* (Mondrian); and to ensure that
mind ruled over matter in such a way that
Beauty became *"the expression of the Soul's
Inner Necessity"*. (Kandinsky).

In the first phase (1910-15), whilst
Kandinsky was seeking in his compositions
to translate the hidden truth of colours
and forms, Mondrian tackled the Vertical-
Horizontal relationship and the three primary
colours (blue, yellow and red). At the
same time, Malevitch was investigating the
"reduction of form to zero" (*Carré noir
sur fond blanc* 1913), which he expressed with
his black squares and crosses on a white
background; he believed, like Mondrian, that
he had developed a technique that broke
definitively with any idea of imitating Nature.

Piet Mondrian
New York City I
1942
oil on canvas 119 × 114

Kasimir Malevitch
Croix noire
Black cross
1915
oil on canvas 80 × 79,5

32

"... we reject volume as an expression of space. Space can no more be measured by volume than liquid can be measured with a ruler. What can space be, other than impenetrable depth? Depth is the only means by which space can be expressed... We are freeing ourselves from the errors of thousands of years of history, errors that began with the Egyptians who maintained that art could only consist in static rhythm. We proclaim that the elements of art originate in dynamic rhythm."

Gabo, Pevsner
Manifeste constructiviste
1920
From the review
*Abstraction-Création
Art Non Figuratif*
Paris 1932 n° 1

1915 marked the beginning of a new period in the history of Abstract Art, characterised by the determination of artists to found a modern "Renaissance."

In Holland, the Mondrian-inspired *De Stijl* movement (1917-28), brought together a group of painters and architects (van Doesburg, Vantongerloo, Rietveld, etc.) to lay the foundations of a shared aesthetic: *Neo-Plasticism.*

In Russia, while Pevsner and Gabo sought the affirmation of a pure *"rhythmic dynamic"* in painting and sculpture, the partisans of *"productive constructivism"* (El Lissitsky, Rodchenko, Tatlin) chose on the contrary to make art objects that would be useful to everyone.

Finally, in Germany, the *Bauhaus* art institute (1919-33), in which Kandinsky, Klee, Moholy-Nagy, etc. participated, combined art and technical accomplishment in the development of collective works (associating architecture, furniture, illustration, theatre and the plastic arts) the first fruits of a new art integrated with industrial society.

This activity was short-lived. After 1933 the ascendancy of Nazism in Germany and of Stalinism in Russia forced many artists to emigrate. This contributed heavily towards making Paris the last capital of Abstract Art in Europe. Founded in 1931, the *Abstraction-Création* group included 400 artists from every country in the world (among others Arp, Delaunay, Herbin, Kupka, Sophie Taeuber-Arp, van Doesburg, Vantongerloo).

Gerrit Rietveld
Armchair
1917
painted wood
87 × 66 × 82

Antoine Pevsner
Masque Mask
1923
celluloid and metal
33 × 20 × 20

Jean Arp
Tête-paysage
1924-26
painted wood
58 × 40 × 4,5

Delaunay's *window* series marked his first attempt at making light itself the subject of his work.

Here the figurative element is reduced to a few minimal indications: the silhouette of the Eiffel Tower (the green crosspieces, above centre), the movement of curtains (suggested by the blue and yellow curves here and there in the middle of the canvas), the façade of a nearby building (below centre). More important is Delaunay's will to express light streaming through window panes, using the full range of colours of the spectrum interwoven in successive planes. The result is a kaleidoscopic effect that seems to shatter the traditional concept of space within a painting.

Robert Delaunay
Une fenêtre
A window
1912-13
oil on canvas 111 × 90

Robert Delaunay
Rythme sans fin
Rhythm without end
1934
oil on canvas 207 × 52

REPRESENTATIONAL ART 1920-30

1905-13 Pascin, Modigliani, Chagall, Kisling, Soutine and Foujita settle at Montparnasse in Paris.

1911-17 André Derain rejects Fauvism and Cubism to draw his inspiration from the "Old Masters".

1916 The ex-Futurist Carlo Carrà calls, in *La Voce* (Florence), for a rediscovery of early Italian painters (Giotto, Uccello, etc.)

1922 Foundation, in Milan, of the *Novecento* group (Sironi, etc.) who recommends a return to the values of the Italian Past.

1926 The "realistic" paintings by Otto Dix, Georg Grosz, and Max Beckmann appear, at the *"Neue Sachlichkeit"* (New Objectivity) exhibition in Mannheim, as a post-war reaction against German Expressionism.

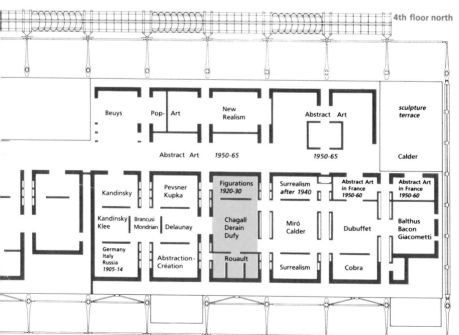

4th floor north

Beuys

Pop- Art

New Realism

Abstract Art

sculpture terrace

Abstract Art   1950-65

1950-65

Calder

Kandinsky

Pevsner Kupka

Figurations 1920-30

Surrealism after 1940

Abstract Art in France 1950-60

Abstract Art in France 1950-60

Kandinsky Klee

Brancusi Mondrian

Delaunay

Chagall Derain Dufy

Miró Calder

Dubuffet

Balthus Bacon Giacometti

Germany Italy Russia 1905-14

Abstraction-Création

Rouault

Surrealism

Cobra

Much frequented by artists in search of
large ateliers, as well as by writers and art-
lovers, Montparnasse between 1910 and 1930
became a rendez-vous for many German,
Japanese (Foujita), and Italian (Modigliani)
painters. But above all the quartier was
a haven for Eastern European artists such as
Kisling, Pascin, Soutine and Chagall, who had
been drawn to Paris by its reputation for
freedom.
These artists, who have since been dubbed
the *Paris School* by art historians, shared
nothing but a deep individualism (which led
each one of them to seek his own very personal
"trademark" style), and a taste for emotive
painting based on the direct expression of
their sensibilities.
Thus the dry graphics of Foujita or Kisling
(tempered by the use of very smooth ingredients), may be contrasted with Modigliani's
soft arabesques; and again there is a world
of difference between the fluid outlines
traced by Pascin, and Soutine's stabbing
brushwork and rough, pasty colours,
which foreshadow the vehement gestures of
the various post-war "Expressionists."

Chaïm Soutine
Le groom
The page-boy
1928
oil on canvas 98 × 80

Amedeo Modigliani
Tête rouge
Red head
1915
oil on cardboard 54 × 42

36

"While participating in this unique technical revolution within French art, I returned to my own country on the wings of thought, so to speak. I lived by turning my back on what was in front of me."

"Our inner world is entirely real, perhaps more real even than the visible world. To call everything that seems illogical a fantasy or a fairy-tale, is to admit that we do not understand nature."

*"Gardens blossom inside me
My flowers are invented,
Some of them belong to me,
But there are no houses
All of them were destroyed in infancy.
The people of my gardens
wander through the air
Looking for a place to stay
They inhabit my soul."*

Mainly quoted
from Marc Chagall
Ma vie
Paris 1931

1887
Birth of Chagall at Vitebsk,
in a strongly religious Jewish milieu.

1910-13
Chagall's first stay in Paris.
Friendship with Cendrars and Appollinaire.
Discovers Cubism.
From 1911, Chagall begins working
with arbitrary "découpage" of figures
so placed as to seem weightless.

1914-22
Returns to Vitebsk. During
the Russian Revolution, Chagall
is commissar of the Vitebsk Beaux-Arts,
then works as a painter of decors
at the Moscow Jewish Theatre.

1922-41
Chagall settles in France. Despite
his sympathy with the Surrealists,
he refuses to join them. Many illustrations of books for the publisher Vollard.

1941-46
Emigration to the United States.

1947-85
Finally settles at Vence and St. Paul,
near Nice. Many mural commissions in France,
Israel, the USA, etc.; stained glass
in the Cathedrals of Metz and Reims,
the ceiling of the Paris Opera, and
the series of paintings of the *Biblical
Message* in Nice.

Marc Chagall
Double portrait au verre de vin
Double portrait with a glass of wine
1917-18
oil on canvas 235 × 137

The work of Rouault, which was much influenced by the Catholic renewal movement after the turn of the century, was unique in Modern Art because of its preoccupation with endowing the Christian message with a new force of expression. Rouault's first pictures, in gouache and aquarelle (1903-14), were Fauvist in their keeness of touch and their search for expressive power. But his representations of broken or pathetic humanity (prostitutes, acrobats) show the fascinated horror and moral anguish with which he viewed *"mankind's hell."* The great series of engravings entitled *Miserere* (1914-27) bear majestic witness to this anguish.

After 1928, Rouault's choice of evangelical themes oriented his work towards the development of more tranquil images. With their structural wealth of symmetry and directness, and with the chromatiç power of their thick colours, his paintings from this period recall the visual intensity of the stained glass of the Middle Ages.

Rouault was an indefatigable craftsman, who considered many of his paintings unfinished. Nine hundred of them, a memorial to the spontaneity of his work, were donated to the Museum by Rouault's family in 1963.

Georges Rouault
La Sainte Face
The Holy Face
1933
oil on canvas 91 × 65

Georges Rouault
L'apprenti ouvrier
The apprentice
c. 1925
oil on canvas 67 × 52

38

While the years between 1905 and 1914 were marked by the founding movements of Modern Art, the shock of the First World War and the social and intellectual upheavals that followed it, led many artists to oppose the aesthetic prejudices of the pre-1914 Avant-Garde. The artists of 1920-30 rejected the theory of the creative self and of a formal break with the past, claiming the right of painting to confront tradition and exterior reality, however disturbing they might prove to be.

Hence, the will to *"scrutinise the visible"* (Max Beckmann), even when it was ugly or banal; and the return to tried and tested techniques of the painter's art, as exemplified by the Old Masters. These were the essential characteristics of the German *New Objectivity* (Beckmann, Dix, Grosz); of the Italian *Novecento* movement (Sironi); and of the French "Classical" and "Realist" movements (Derain, Gruber, etc.).

Coldness and irony were the hallmarks of this period. Even the deliberately academic quality of the painting emphasises (for the first time in modern art) the anxiety of a generation for which Modernity was beginning to mean the revelation of the world's *"disturbing alienation"* from itself (De Chirico).

Mario Sironi
Lac de montagne
Mountain lake
1928
oil on canvas 60 × 71

André Derain
Nature morte aux oranges
Still life with oranges
1931
oil on canvas 89 × 117

Portrait of the journalist Sylvia von Harden
1926

Otto Dix met Sylvia von Harden, a pictu-
resque figure in Berlin in the 1920's, at the Café
Romain, much patronised by artists at that time.
The visual shock produced by his resultant
portrait of her, derives from the contrast between
the caricature of an emancipated woman and
the smooth, detached treatment she receives.
Because of this quality (and also because of the
technique used—glazing and wood support)
Otto Dix's portrait seems as ageless and impassive
as those of the great German Masters (Lucas
Cranach, Hans Baldung Grien), whose successor
he sought to be.

Otto Dix
Bildnis der journalistin Sylvia von Harden
Portrait of the journalist Sylvia von Harden
1926
oil on wood 121 × 89

DADA SURREALISM

1910-17 Giorgio De Chirico's *Metaphysical Paintings*.

1913-17 Marcel Duchamp's first *Ready-Mades*.

1916 Foundation of the *Dada* movement in Zurich by Hans Arp, Hugo Ball, Richard Huelsenbeck, Marcel Janco, Tristan Tzara.

1917-22 *Dada* manifestations in Berlin, Cologne, Hanover, New York, Paris.

1924 *Manifeste du Surréalisme* by André Breton. First issue of *La Révolution Surréaliste (Aragon, Breton, Desnos, Eluard, Naville, Péret, etc.)*.

1925 First exhibition of Surrealist paintings in Paris. (Arp, De Chirico, Ernst, Klee, Man Ray, Masson, Miró, Picasso, Pierre Roy).

1930 First number of *Le Surréalisme au service de la Révolution*. Breton and his friends join the French Communist Party (1927-33).

1938 The international Surrealist exhibition in Paris. 60 artists from 40 different countries.

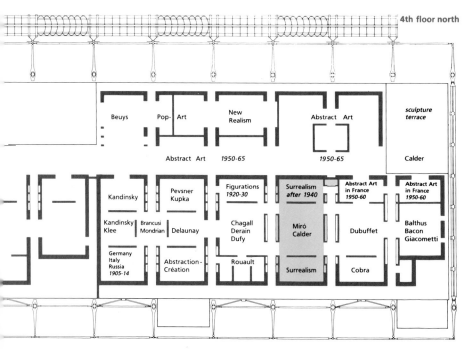

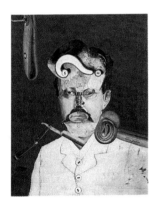

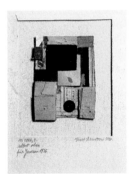

Dada was foreshadowed between 1913 and 1915 by the iconoclastic investigations of Duchamp, Picabia and Man Ray in New York, but it was not until 1916 in Zurich that the movement came to full fruition, under the impetus of a general disgust at the horrors of the First World War. *Dada* (a word picked haphazardly from the dictionary) was above all a revolt among intellectuals confronted with the spectacle of the collapse of European civilisation. Its authors rejected ordinary values, which had anyway been belied by the war, and questioned the validity of autonomous artistic endeavour. Dada set out to reveal the complete inanity of these things by a campaign of provocation and by the fabrication of works that were deliberately preposterous or absurd—it affirmed, by contrast, the need to struggle for the emancipation of the individual from all social constraints.

This multi-faceted creative activity led Dada to invent a new status for the "objet d'art," by divesting it of any pre-established aesthetic character. This was to be accomplished in two ways: by *"promoting manufactured objects to the dignity of works of art"* (Marcel Duchamp's *ready-mades*) and by the creation of random forms through play, derision and the spontaneous association of ideas (*collages, constructions* and *photomontages* by Grosz, Hausmann, Schwitters, etc.).

Kurt Schwitters
Merz 1926,2
1926
collage on cardboard 12,5 × 9,5
with cardboard 35 × 26

George Grosz
Remember uncle August, the unhappy inventor
1919
oil, pencil and collage on canvas 49 × 39

Man Ray
Cadeau Gift
1921-63
iron and nails
(original of 1963 from the lost model)
17,5 × 10 × 14

42

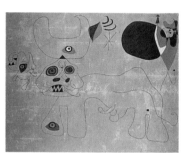

Miró discovered Surrealism in Paris between 1920 and 1924, through his neighbour in the next studio, André Masson. He took the decision to *"go beyond the plastic thing"* and began to develop a form of *"poetry-painting,"* drawing on a store of images from his dreams. With their graphic improvisations (letters, numbers, wandering or stippled lines) and with their unexpected juxtapositions of elementary signs, (small figures, fantastic animals, starry skies), Miró's *"mi-hié-ro-glyphes"* (as Raymond Queneau called them), are reminiscent of the indefinable blend of joy and tension that we see in the art work of children and primitive peoples.

By 1930, Miró was *"out to murder painting."* He tried a number of technical experiments (painting on copper, sandpaper, and masonite), and embarked on the construction of objects out of scrap material. Later, between 1944 and 1959, he devoted himself mainly to ceramics, sculpture and mural decoration.

Miró's return to painting, which took place after 1960, took the form of very large canvasses with stains of colour and print marks. This development shows that the artist remained faithful to the ideal he had set himself: *"to achieve maximum intensity with a minimum of ingredients."*

Joan Miró
L'addition
The addition
1925
oil and paste on pasted canvas 195 × 129

Joan Miró
La course de taureaux
Bullfight
1945
oil on canvas 114 × 144

Which has influenced you more, nature or
modern machinery?
*Nature. I haven't really touched machinery
except for a few elementary mechanisms like
levers and balances. You see nature and then
you try to emulate it.*

How did the mobiles start?
*The mobiles started when I went to see
Mondrian. I was impressed by several colored
rectangles he had on the wall. Shortly after
that I made some mobiles; Mondrian claimed
his paintings were faster than my mobiles.*

How do your mobiles differ from your stabiles
in intention?
*Well, the mobile has actual movement in
itself, while the stabile is back at the old
painting idea of implied movement. You have
to walk around a stabile or through it—a
mobile dances in front of you.*

How do you feel about your motorized
mobiles?
*The motorized ones are too painful—too
many mechanical bugaboos (...).*

Alexander Calder
Extracts from an interview by Katharine Kuh
in The Artist's Voice
New York 1960

Alexander Calder
Shark and whale
c. 1933
wood 98 × 102 × 16

Alexander Calder
White disc, black disc
1940-41
painted wood, sheet metal,
wire, motor 124 × 92 × 45

43

44

"Surrealism: pure psychic automatism, by which a person seeks to express, either verbally or in writing or in any other way, the real functioning of his thought. Dictated by thought, in the absence of any control exerted by reason, independent of any aesthetic or moral constraint."

André Breton
Manifeste du Surréalisme

René Magritte
Le modèle rouge
The red model
1935
oil on canvas pasted on cardboard 56 × 46

When transposed to the plastic arts, this descent towards the source of inspiration —the subconscious— provides an equivalent to literary automatism in techniques which can play the part of *"optical agitators"* (Max Ernst). These are: automatic drawing, *collages* of illustrations or objects juxtaposed for purely emotive reasons, *rubbings*, taken by the use of a pencil on a piece of paper laid against a rough surface (Max Ernst), or sand thrown against canvasses covered in fresh glue (Masson). Such techniques conjure up vague images, which *"provoke a sudden intensification of the visionary faculties"* (Max Ernst). At the same time, traditional representative art, even the *trompe-l'œil*, allows the fixation of hallucinatory images, which constitute so many *"dream tracings"* (Dali). Finally, objects found, interpreted, assembled, and diverted, constitute for the Surrealists the ultimate means of emancipation from the mental confinement of the image. Thus it is no longer towards literature, painting and sculpture that Surrealism opens up new perspectives, but towards a poetic region which is beyond all of them, in which there is *"total liberation of the spirit and of everything else that resembles it"* (André Breton).

Joseph Cornell
Owl box
1945-46
assemblage 63 × 36 × 16

Giorgio De Chirico
Portrait prémonitoire de Guillaume Apollinaire
1914
oil on canvas 81 × 65

Loplop presents a young girl
1930-66

The "Loplop presents" series appeared
in Max Ernst's work between 1929 and 1934.
Loplop the bird, a trademark for the artist,
exhibited small paintings, collages, rubbings or
photomontages, often very carefully framed.
In this way Loplop achieved a kind of double
identity for the artist and his work.

The "young woman" here "presented" is
thus a work within a work, a collage on a
wooden panel taken from among the props used
in Luis Buñuel's film "L'Age d'Or." The collage is
made up of objects associated with the "visions"
induced in the artist as he observed the painted
plaster reliefs on the panel. Perhaps the work
began as a sarcastic allusion to the sentimental
objects preserved in lockets. In its first version
(1930), it simply consisted of a young girl's
profile, a lock of hair and a few ribbons. After
these came the lid of the wash boiler, the pebble
in the net, the little plaster mask (1936), and
finally the bronze frog (1966). As a "cultivation of
the effects of systematic alienation" (Max Ernst),
the full force of the collage is present here: it is
the force of the irrational, which is to say, of
desire.

Max Ernst
A l'intérieur de la vue
Inside Sight
1929
oil on canvas 100 × 81

Max Ernst
Loplop présente une jeune fille
Loplop presents a young girl
1930-66
mixed media on board 194 × 89 × 10

46

—If Tanguy was a colour,
what would it be?
—A fresh, vivid yellow,
a little voice tells me.
(...)
—And if Tanguy was a complex?
—It would be a guilt complex.
(...)
—Or a gem?
—Erotic drop earrings.
(...)
—An element?
—The air.
(...)
—Seafood?
—A barnacle.
(...)
—Perversion?
—Sadism.
(...)
—A particular hour of the day?
—Four or five o'clock in the morning.
(...)
—A toilet article?
—A hairbrush.
(...)
—A primitive people?
—The Jivaros.
(...)
—A form of mental illness?
—Alternating bouts of euphoria
and depression.
(...)
—A torture?
—The Chinese water torture.
(...)
—A superstition?
—Spilt salt.
(...)

Benjamin Peret *Yves Tanguy
ou l'anatife torpille les Jivaros*
from Cahiers d'art
Paris, 1935
volume X n°s 5-6

Yves Tanguy
A quatre heures d'été, l'espoir
Summer at four, hope
1929
oil on canvas 129 × 97

Surrealism, first made known by the works
of Miró and Picasso during the 1920's found
a new echo in the United States following the
arrival around 1940 as immigrants of Breton,
Ernst, Masson and Matta, who familiarised the
young artists of New York with the techniques
of automatism. The appearance of fluid forms,
"biomorphic," as in Gorky's paintings, which
sometimes had totemic or mythical overtones,
(Pollock), was a characteristic of this new
school. American Surrealism rapidly acquired
an individuality of its own through a strong
emphasis on exploring new techniques such as
drip-painting[1], in which automatism became
a plastic tool for gestural expression on a more
and more monumental scale.

[1] See *short dictionary
of American Abstract Art*
pages 54-55.

Arshile Gorky
Landscape-Table
1945
oil on canvas 92 × 121

André Masson
Les villageois
The villagers
1927
oil and sand on canvas 81 × 65

REPRESENTATIONAL AND ABSTRACT ART 1935-65

1922	First "blot paintings" by Hans Hartung in Dresden.
1934	First Balthus exhibition in Paris.
1935	Giacometti breaks with Surrealism; returns to life studies.
1944-45	Dubuffet, Fautrier, Wols exhibitions in Paris.
1946	Foundation of the *Salon des Réalités nouvelles* in Paris, dedicated to Abstract Art.
1947	First Jackson Pollock *Drip-Paintings* in USA.
1948	Founding of *Cobra* in Paris.
1958	First Frank Stella *Stripe-Paintings* in USA.

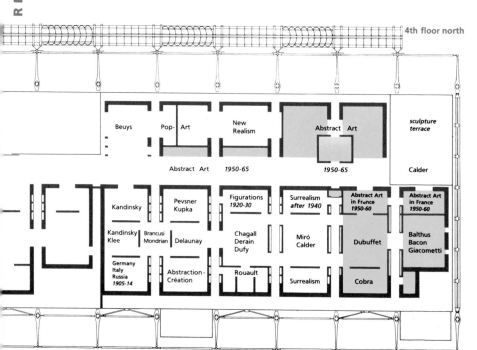

4th floor north

Beuys Pop-Art New Realism Abstract Art sculpture terrace

Abstract Art 1950-65 1950-65 Calder

Kandinsky Pevsner Kupka Figurations 1920-30 Surrealism after 1940 Abstract Art in France 1950-60 Abstract Art in France 1950-60

Kandinsky Klee Brancusi Mondrian Delaunay Chagall Derain Dufy Miró Calder Dubuffet Balthus Bacon Giacometti

Germany Italy Russia 1905-14 Abstraction-Création Rouault Surrealism Cobra

In 1942, Dubuffet made his final decision to break with what he called *"our suffocating culture,"* and to seek inspiration in the *"common man's"* freshness of expression—as exemplified by street graffiti and spontaneous daubing. Using instinctive lines, ground up materials and elementary figures, Dubuffet thenceforward associated himself with the search for *"the ancestral spontaneity of the human hand drawing symbols."* This commitment resulted in human portraits of extreme crudeness (*Dhôtel nuancé d'abricot* 1947), "landscapes" made out of ordinary soils reconstituted for the purpose, (*Le voyageur sans boussole* 1952), and the foundation in 1948 of the *Compagnie de l'Art brut*, which collected the artwork of people supposed by society to be mad or simple-minded. All Dubuffet's work prior to 1963 was dedicated to proving a single point, that *"art is always to be found where you least expect it."*

Jean Dubuffet
Le voyageur sans boussole, 8 juillet 1952
Traveller without a compass, July 8th 1952
1952
oil on masonite 118 × 155

Jean Dubuffet
Dhôtel nuancé d'abricot
Portrait of André Dhôtel in shades of apricot
1947
oil on canvas 116 × 89

50

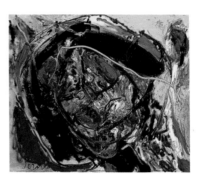

Cobra was founded in Paris by Asger Jorn, a Dane, Christian Dotremont, a Belgian and Karel Appel, Constant and Corneille, all three of whom were Dutch. The name *"COBRA"* (COpenhagen, BRussels, Amsterdam) is an amalgam of initials from the cities of origin of its founders. The idea was to rediscover *"experimental, simplistic art"* by *"the living agency of the painter, the spontaneous vitality of matter and the dialectic of inner life and objective existence."*

Between 1948 and 1951, Cobra's spheres of interest were extended to poetry, architecture and cinema, along with every form of Northern European folk art. But painting always held pride of place among the group's members; and here the free juxtaposition of abstract techniques (interlaces, smears and stains) with monstrous animals and primitive figures, produced a deliberately "brutal" effect. This was heightened by the use of violent, urgent colours, applied with the palette knife on every kind of surface.

Cobra was anti-aesthetic and anti-rationalist; it sought to rehabilitate creativity in its most spontaneous form, in contrast to the artistic formalism that characterised the epoch.

Karel Appel
Vragende Kinderen
Questioning children
1948
oil on wood assemblage 85 × 56

Asger Jorn
Femme du 5 octobre
1958
oil on canvas 63 × 76

"*All modern artists work within the same framework, which is their yearning to seize and possess something which perpetually escapes them,*" said Giacometti during a 1962 interview.

Yet the modern artist also knows he can only seize that "*something which escapes*", that elusive reality, by "*copying appearances.*" thus Giacometti concentrates his figures in more and more emaciated and denser forms in order to express the life they contain. The overall effect, in his own words, is to "*hollow out a vacuum around them.*" Balthus, using a different method, petrifies visions that are familiar to all of us, making them seem like theatrical scenes peopled by frozen actors in artificial poses.

"*It's as though reality were always hidden behind curtains which one draws aside*" —another quote from Giacometti. With Bacon the drawn curtains reveal agonising images, ravaged faces, contorted bodies lost in abstract infinity. They are presented thus, says Michel Leiris "*... as though the reality of life could only be encapsulated in the form of a scream, a scream of truth, one could say; and this scream, if it does not come from the thing itself, must be that of the artist, possessed by a mania to grasp and comprehend*".

Francis Bacon
Portrait de Michel Leiris
1976
oil on canvas 34 × 29

Alberto Giacometti
Femme debout II
Woman standing II
1959-60
bronze 275 × 55 × 33

"The longer I looked at the model, the thicker the screen between its reality and myself became (...) I mean that in 1940, the heads became tiny, almost vanishing completely. All I could distinguish were millions of details. In order to see these details united in a whole, I had to move the model further and further away. The further away it was, the smaller the head became; this filled me with terror. The danger of things disappearing..."

Alberto Giacometti
extract from an interview with A. Parinaud
in Arts
Paris, June 1962

"... the picture is not pure contemplation, but its simulacrum, and this is why the life frozen on its surface has such fascination. The picture has no being as such, but, thanks to the "non-being" of its simulacrum-function, it does enable us to see the very being within which things can no longer die because they are no longer living: they are. It is not so much that the picture offers us an object for contemplation, as that it causes us to wait for the spectacle of that which we are already looking at, but which will be animated by intermediary demons between the artist and the spectator."

Pierre Klossowski
Balthus beyond realism
from Art News, New York
1956, vol. 55 n° 8

Alberto Giacometti
Portrait d'Isaku Yanaïhara
1956
oil on canvas 81 × 65

Balthus
La chambre turque
The Turkish room 1963-66
casein tempera with marble powder
on canvas 180 × 210

Between 1945 and 1960, Abstract Art became the dominant mode of expression within European Art. At the same time it was geared down into a number of proliferating schools, frequently at odds with one another. Thus *Geometric Abstract* (Dewasne, Herbin, Magnelli) quickly found fresh application in the aesthetics of movement (Soto, Schöffer) and optical variations on a flat surface (Agam, Vasarely). In contrast to this was the French tradition of the *Poetic Abstract* (Bazaine, de Stael, Esteve); as well as the *Lyrical Abstract*, which favoured stains and spots (Bryen), graphism (Hartung, Soulages), signs (Michaux); and even the convulsive separation of all forms (Wols' *Informal Art*).

By using such ingredients as blanc d'Espagne whitening and glue (Fautrier), old canvas sacking (Burri), pulverised marble and latex (Tapiès) or even tar, sand and organic waste (Dubuffet), these painters embarked on a painstaking exploration of Matter.

Parallel to these European trends, the American *Abstract Expressionists* (Pollock, Newman, Rothko) concentrated on developing and refining the creative act itself (*Action-Painting*); they sought to involve the spectator directly in the emotive power of colour (*Color-Field Painting*) by the use of monumental forms which sometimes resulted in the creation of true picture "environments".

Nicolas de Staël
De la danse
1946
oil on canvas 195 × 114

Jean Fautrier
Femme douce
Gentle woman
1946
mixed media on canvas 97 × 145

Victor Vasarely
Hô II
1948-52
oil on canvas 130 × 81

Action Painting   Rapid pictorial technique whereby the artist expresses his deepest impulses directly on canvas. Jackson Pollock, Willem de Kooning and Mark Tobey are the chief exponents of Action Painting, which seeks to eliminate any differentiation between drawing and painting by use of "physical automatism." The technique achieves open forms, inseparable from the space containing them, in which the creative act is reflected exactly as it is by the completed work.

All-Over   Pictorial space without beginning or end, created by Jackson Pollock in his *"Drip-paintings"*. Here the eye is made to rove around in all directions, because the canvas contains no central focus or point of reference.

Willem de Kooning
Woman
c. 1952
crayon and charcoal on paper
two assembled drawings 74 × 50

Barnett Newman
Shining forth (to George)
1961
oil on canvas 290 × 442

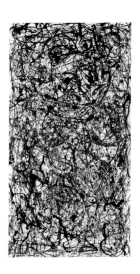

Color-Field Painting   Painting by "fields of intense colour" which unite to build a single, infinitely extendable image, the shape of which is derived from the canvas itself. Color-Field Painting has produced real "abstract icons" such as Mark Rothko's blurred rectangles or Barnett Newman's rhythmic vertical stripes (*Shining Forth* 1961). These are "sense-symbols" of the artist's confrontation with space.

Drip-Painting or Dripping   This process involves dripping paint on a canvas laid flat on the floor, using boxes of fluid colour pierced full of holes. Max Ernst experimented with "Drip-Painting" in 1942, the technique was systematised by Jackson Pollock after 1947 and eventually resulted in the creation of *All-Over* paintings.

Hard Edge   Geometrical Abstract Art movement, started towards the end of the 1950's (by Ellsworth Kelly, Kenneth Noland, etc.), in which the colour scheme of the painting is given prominence by the use of zones of intense colour with sharply-defined contours. Frank Stella's work contains the same urge to reduce the work of art to its basic essentials. Stella began with stripe paintings and went on after 1960 to cut up his pictures around the edges of the forms they contained; his purpose in doing this was simply to emphasize their existence. Stella said of these works *"What you see is what you see."*

Frank Stella
Parzeczew II
1971
acrylic on canvas, cardboard and felt
on wood 270 × 261

Jackson Pollock
Number 26 A, Black and White
1948
enamel on canvas 205 × 122

NEW REALISM POP ART FLUXUS

1954 Rauschenberg creates his first *Combine-Paintings* in New York.

1956 Exhibition *This is to-morrow* in London.

1958 First *Happenings* in New York.

1960 Foundation of the *New Realists* group in Paris. (Arman, César, Klein, Raysse, Spoerri, Tinguely, Villeglé, etc.).

1962 Consecration of *Pop Art* in the USA. First *Fluxus* concerts in Europe.

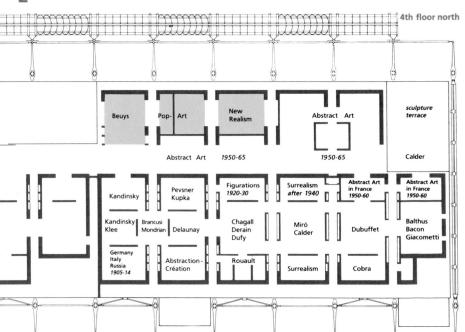

4th floor north

Beuys	Pop- Art	New Realism	Abstract Art	sculpture terrace
	Abstract Art	1950-65	1950-65	Calder
Kandinsky	Pevsner Kupka	Figurations 1920-30	Surrealism after 1940	Abstract Art in France 1950-60	Abstract Art in France 1950-60
Kandinsky Klee	Brancusi Mondrian	Delaunay	Chagall Derain Dufy	Miró Calder	Dubuffet	Balthus Bacon Giacometti
Germany Italy Russia 1905-14	Abstraction-Création		Rouault	Surrealism	Cobra	

The *New.Realists* gave artistic value to the appropriation of everyday objects for use by artists, which in effect endowed them with an aesthetic quality stemming from the simple fact of their choice. This led them to undertake a general salvage of modern reality, a kind of reinterpretation of Marcel Duchamp's "ready-made" art after their own fashion.

This rediscovery of industrial and urban folklore mostly took the form of series artwork, in which objects were accumulated, smashed (Arman), wrapped (Christo), compressed (César) or fixed wherever they happened to be (Spœrri's *"trapped objects,"* or torn posters by Hains and Villeglé). They were also poetic assemblages of "marvellous modernity," such as the junk assemblages constructed by Niki de St. Phalle or Martial Raysse.

In a more general sense, this reconquest of the world changes into an all-round approach by which the artist appropriates not only objects but also movement, noise, energy (as in Tinguely's machines), even cosmic space (as "materialised" by Yves Klein's blue *monochromes*). Thus New Realist Art, with its often spectacular results, becomes the "total art" medium, permeating the universe with what Yves Klein has called *"indefinable, immaterial pictorial sensibility"*.

"... I think painting is invisible. It's absolutely indefinable and invisible, it's impalpable, and yet it's present. It's a presence, it inhabits a place or an area, and as far as I'm concerned, my painting currently inhabits this gallery, but I'd like it to assume almost immeasurable dimensions, to spread out and impregnate the atmosphere of a whole town, maybe even a whole country..."

Yves Klein
interview on radio Europe 1
on his exhibition *"The Void"*
Paris 1958
quoted in the Yves Klein catalogue
Centre Georges Pompidou
Paris 1983

Arman
Home Sweet Home
1960
accumulation of gas masks
160 × 140 × 20

Yves Klein
Monochrome IKB 3
IKB 3 blue monochrome
1960
dry pigment in synthetic resin on fabric,
mounted on board 199 × 153

"There is no reason for us not to believe that the whole world is a gigantic painting." This remark by the American painter Rauschenberg encapsulates the behaviour of a generation of artists, particularly American artists, who found themselves confronted by the visual explosion of the consumer society into ordinary life.

Pop (short for popular) Art set its heart on everyday banality, which it either reproduced or utilised directly by employing its most commonplace elements—as in the "painted assemblages" of Rauschenberg or Jim Dine, the "environments" of Kienholz or Segal, and Oldenburg's "sculpture objects." Another Pop Art technique was to "monumentalize" the images produced by advertising (Rosenquist), strip cartoons (Lichtenstein), or mass reader-ship newspapers (Warhol).

By working, as Rauschenberg said, "in the gap that separates art from life," Pop Art reintroduced "objectivity of vision" to painting, and unburdened it of any pictorial illusionism. The eye, which is drawn back to the object re-produced or to the ready-made image being re-presented, discovers both the detached nature of reality and the sheer expressionist potential of its representation. Pop Art neither glorifies nor denigrates its epoch, and hence it can bring to bear another kind of objective detachment: humour. In this sense Pop Art's message is both aesthetic and moral.

Jasper Johns
Figure 5
1960
encaustic and newsprint on canvas
183 × 137

Andy Warhol
Electric Chair
1966
acrylic and silkscreen enamel
on canvas 137 × 185

Happenings were originally conceived as a meeting of all the forms of artistic expression[1]. The idea was to substitute action for the art object, public participation for passive contemplation and uncertainty for certainty. Allan Kaprow, Jim Dine and Claes Oldenburg initiated the first Happenings in New York from 1958 onwards; they produced theatrical, neo-Dadaist games with improvised scenarios that took place in ephemeral, endlessly modifiable "environments" associating objects, sounds and spectator reactions.

Between 1962 and 1963, the movement spread to Europe by the agency of Georges Maciunas, who organised concerts to experiment with *"the state of flux to which all art forms can be traced."* The *Fluxus concerts*, as they were known, brought together artists such as George Brecht, Robert Filliou, Wolf Vostell and Nam June Paik; the concert were intended to demonstrate the potential of unexpected actions and gestures; these were variously called *"compositions,"* *"performances,"* or *"events."* They showed that art was capable of loosening the stranglehold of commerce and culture in order to become accessible to all. The *Happenings* were intended to bring art closer to play and magic — in short, closer to life.

After 1964, the traces left by the Fluxus activities, such as publications, letters, photographs, films, etc., were channelled into the Art market.

[1] According to the theories propounded after 1952 by the composer John Cage

"It is a state of nature, a condition, that I want to represent above all, the large formal realm of softness, which one's own body suggests. (...) Only hard originals are taken as subject for softening. Softening may be seen as pacifist wish fulfillment (soft car, soft gun), endless staying in bed, pleasure, as championing drugged impotence, transvestism, melting of barriers, subversion, as anti-ambition, as the projection of body, of author's body, or calling attention to the great neglected formal realm of the non-rigid (airship). Whatever is required, soft is generous. The last act, of softening the thing, is like a climax, a death blow to its functionality and classicism. The object is reduced to nature, left a heap. Its soul, one may say, rises to the heaven of things in the "ghost" form. Its exorcised spirit returns to the realm of geometry leaving a pile of wrinkled laundry. Christian Science. Amen."

Claes Oldenburg
Object into Monument
Pasadena Art Museum
California 1972

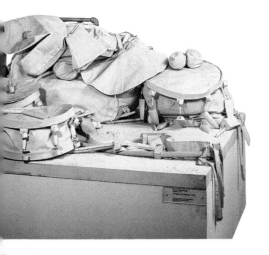

Claes Oldenburg
Ghost drum set
1972
canvas filled with polystyrene balls and painted
80 × 183 × 183

Joseph Beuys

Infiltration homogen for grand piano
1966

1 *"The most important thing for people who look at my objects is my fundamental thesis: EVERYONE OF US IS AN ARTIST. "*

Joseph Beuys

Beuys, a one-time travelling companion of Fluxus, later became linked to the German Ecology movement. His own work is accomplished during public sessions in which he seeks to broaden the frontiers of art and give it an anthropological and collective dimension[1].

By the use of natural substances such as wood, greases, honey and felt, along with instruments and materials produced by technological civilisation, Beuys attempts to reconstruct the unities which have been broken by modern society (Mind-Matter, Nature-Culture, Collectivity-Individual, East-West) and to draw attention to the emotional content of their plastic and ideological oppositions (soft-hard, vague-precise, chaotic-organised).

Here, a concert piano, which symbolises spirituality, has been sewn up by Beuys inside a felt skin, which is an organic symbol of insulation (hence of blocked communication) but also of preservation.

The piano is paralysed and condemned to silence; it seems endangered (note the red crosses on its sides), but its potential remains protected and intact. Its muffled appeal—sound *"filtered"* through felt—as Beuys describes it, is an alarm signal; the piano's tragedy is echoed by the world outside, racked as it is by the birth pangs of an uncertain future.

Joseph Beuys
Infiltration homogen für Konzertflügel
1966
piano covered with felt
100 × 152 × 240

In the galleries of the 3rd floor, are housed the collections of contemporary art.

There, are organized temporary shows of works by living artists of the last two generations. The only permanent exhibits are the *Winter garden* by Jean Dubuffet and Ben's *Store*. Other pieces cited or reproduced hereafter may be temporarily removed.

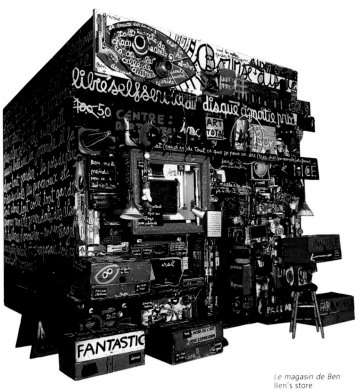

Le magasin de Ben
Ben's store
1958-73
materials and objects from his store in Nice
350 × 500 × 350

CONTEMPORARY ART AFTER 1965

1963 The Korean Nam June Paik exhibits his first "diverted" television images at Cologne.

1963-66 First *Minimal Art* exhibitions in New York.

1967 Formation of the first *Conceptual Art* group in New York (Robert Barry, Douglas Huebler, Joseph Kosuth, Lawrence Weiner).
First *Arte Povera* exhibitions in Italy.
First *Land Art* operations in the United States.

1969 International confrontation of *Process Art, Land Art, Arte Povera* and *Conceptual Art* at an exhibition entitled "When attitudes become form", in Bern.

1970 First *Supports/Surfaces* exhibition in Paris.

1980 Official consecration of German Neo-Fauvism (Baselitz, Kiefer) at the Venice Biennale. The critic Bonito-Oliva baptizes as *"Trans avant-garde"* the figurative renewal movement in Italy.

3rd floor south

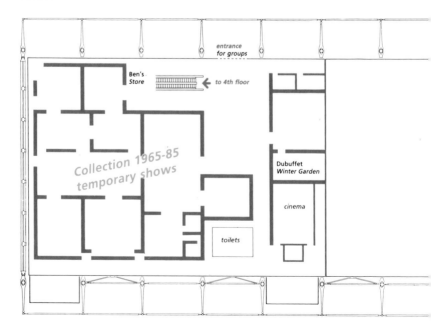

entrance for groups

Ben's Store

← to 4th floor

Collection 1965-85 temporary shows

Dubuffet Winter Garden

cinema

toilets

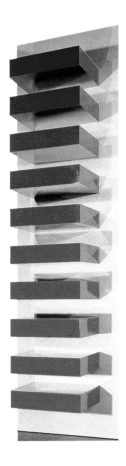

The Minimal Art movement in the United States set out to demonstrate the essential qualities of Painting (two-dimensionality and colour) and Sculpture (three-dimensionality) under the influence of the *Hard Edge* movement[1]. This was achieved by developing *"specific objects"* with radically simplified forms. The theory behind this action was a rejection of artistic virtuosity and of any representational or symbolic function attached to the work of art as such.

After 1965, *Minimal Art* mainly fulfilled its purpose through sculpture, with the use of series combinations of geometrical modular elements of wood, metal or luminous tubes to overcome spatial reality. Most of these elements were of industrial manufacture. With them, forms became *"arrangements"* which affirmed the force of their presence (Don Judd's lines of boxes), or the occupation of a place (Carl André's floor assemblages, Don Flavin's fluorescent lighting) or even the pure *"manifestation of an idea"* (Sol Lewitt's structures derived from a square projected and multiplied in space).

This school is often called anti-emotional (*"Cool Art"*) because of its conspicuous freedom from rhetoric. Nonetheless, its smooth surfaces and clear volumes express the rigour of a form of art which seeks its only justification within itself.

[1] See *Short dictionary of American Abstract Art,* pages 54-55.

Don Judd
Stack
1973
stainless steel and plexiglass
10 units, each 23,5 × 102,5 × 80
with 23 cm intervals

64

"When I make little objects
out of cardboard I work like
a real painter, with emotions
and desires. There is an element
of chance, too. But the photography stage is completely
separate and detached, much
more intellectual, even though
my photographs look like
paintings.
Photography enables me to
really play around with the
medium, by which I mean I can
record extremely ephemeral
events. On the other hand, the
objects aren't exhibited to the
public; they're nothing in
themselves. You've seen them,
they're totally miserable-looking
things; but here's a time lapse
of a few seconds during which
the lighting and dramatisation
of these objects gives them a
certain presence. Photography
provides the only proof of that
fleeting moment. (...) But what
is even more interesting about
photography is it allows me to
use two codes. The high code,
the "painting-type" code, is
almost religious, very impres-
sive, often with grand totemic
characters. The low code is
a "photo" code: it says these
people aren't gods, they're little
toys—this isn't painting, it's photography, which is a lesser art.
At the same time, my photos
are pure photos because they're
souvenirs of an event.
And they're not photos at all,
because they're not in the least
bit naturalistic"

Christian Boltanski
The shadow artist
Extract from an interview
by Michel Nuridsany
in Art Press
Paris, March 1984 n° 79

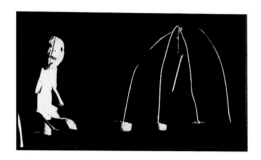

"A medium which is incapable of
distinguishing reality from its reflection...
what are we to think of its pretensions to
authenticity?"[1] This is the question which
accompanies today's renewal of photography
as a "pictorial" medium, because when
we look at the various rules of photography
(objectivity, representation, narration),
the same problems can be said to
apply to painting.
What laws of perspective? asks Jan Dibbets,
for example, with his photographs of
landscapes tilted from 6° to 72°, which
look like the ascending curve of a comet.
What statement? is the implication of Jochen
Gerz, whose enigmatic pictures have titles
that explain nothing about them.
Proof of what? insinuates Jean Le Gac, when
he chooses to illustrate his wandering
autobiography with soothing pictures of the
places he frequents, and illustrations from
children's books.
  Boyd Webb or William Wegman show the
drama involved in photographic perception—
but what does the camera's cold eye perceive?
Aberrant scenes, improbable juxtapositions of
objects which have no logical connection. Not
far off, Gilbert and George physically inhabit
their own photomontages to represent the
right-thinking English middle-class. But what
would their mimed emotions look like if they
were embalmed in the windows of a church?
They are merely *"images of images,"* in which
"everyone can recognise himself" (Christian
Boltanski, talking about his *"Compositions")*,
and from which childish improvisations seem
to emerge by magic from the impalpable night
of memory.

Christian Boltanski
Composition grotesque
Ludicrous composition
1981
photography 109 × 193,5

[1] Edmund Kuppel.

From 1967 onwards, *Conceptual Art* started to question the content and function of Art, instead of its forms. This produced a wide range of research within the framework of a reflexive problem at odds with prevailing formalist attitudes. For this reason, the first medium favoured for the analysis of *"Art as idea as idea"* (Joseph Kosuth[1]) or for the "dematerialisation" of Art[2], was Language—in the form of photographed or painted texts.

Later, during the 1970's, other initiatives which utilised both the highest "technology" and craftsmanship on the smallest scale, allowed a further broadening of the field of research. This research involved questioning the visual rules of the game as well as Art's pretended neutrality in economic, social and political matters.

Thus Marcel Broodthaer's "word-images" lead us to confront our own cultural representations with the immensity of their possible significance, while Nam June Paik's *"hotch-potch of video images"* (achieved by diverting television programmes), Barbara Kruger's disturbing photomontages or Jenny Holzer's cold *"truisms"* moving across an electronic display screen, offer art a different role in the ideological universe governed by the mass media. This role consists of shuffling the cards.

Daniel Buren's uniformly striped canvasses are created in the same spirit. His aim is to broaden the spectators vision of surrounding reality; it is up to the spectator to grasp the fact that the only sense of this anonymous *"visual tool"* is to reveal the environment he occupies, (and which indeed is trying to efface itself from his mind). In short, the purpose of Buren's art is to *"criticize reality, evaluate it, contradict it and subject it to dialectical analysis"* (Daniel Buren).

[1] For example, by confronting objects with their photographic likenesses and dictionary definitions.

[2] By substituting allusive written propositions which are left to the reader's imagination (Lawrence Weiner, Robert Barry, etc.).

Marcel Broodthaers
Le corbeau et le renard
The crow and the fox
1968
photographic canvas and typewriter
115 × 82

Daniel Buren
Ornements d'un discours
Figures of speech
1973-78
striped canvas - 1 piece 90 × 141
and 36 small pieces 10 × 17 each

66

What is the meaning of the verb "to perceive"? For an artist, attempting an answer to this question is to cease considering the work of art as a finished object, in order to open himself to the dynamic of realisation and setting.

In this way, art becomes an experimental *"active force"*[1] which can use any material, hard or soft, to demonstrate the creative process[2] and its visualisation in the finished work.

Thus, when Richard Serra bespatters a wall with molten lead and builds dangerous "houses of cards" with precariously balanced sheets of steel, or when Robert Ryman paints his "white" pictures by concentrating his full attention on spreading the pigment over various types of supports (paper, canvas, metal, plexiglass) and on fixing the supports to the wall[3], these artists are inviting the onlooker to share the intensity of their sensory experience.

Italian *Arte Povera* seeks to rediscover the deeper man who is *"reintegrated with the cosmic energy of things"* (Luciano Fabro), particularly with the energy of those objects and substances which are farthest from conventional artistic codes (untreated wool, lettuce leaves, ground coffee, stuffed animals). This is achieved by the revelation of their hidden character. Hence the artist is viewed as a newly-arrived nomad and predator, who captures the life buried away under the ground or in the plants, the secret strength of earth's magnetic force. His territory is an "igloo" of sacks filled with earth.

By extending its domain into the cities, the countryside and the wilderness, *Land Art* takes the whole planet as its field of experiment. Of his meditative arrangements of stones and branches collected during walks in the country, Richard Long says: *"My work is about real stones, real time, and real actions."*

[1] The expression used by the Italian artist Piero Manzoni.

[2] Hence the term *Process Art* (or *Anti-Form*) used by American critics.

[3] *"The problem is not what to paint, but how to paint."*
Robert Ryman

Robert Ryman
Chapter
1981
oil on linen with metal 223,5 × 213,4

Mario Merz
Igloo di Giap
Giap's Igloo
1968
iron carcass, earth bags,
neon tubes 120 × 200

Conceived as an inventory of "the work of making" using the traditional ingredients of painting (canvasses, frames and pigments), the activity of the *Supports/Surfaces* group in France (1970-71) drew attention to the kind of multiple but convergent work initiated by Simon Hantaï. Since 1960, the latter had been painting on folded or wrinkled canvasses which he deployed just as they were and impregnated with colours.

In 1966, Claude Viallat began to work with repetitive prints of colours made with stencils or brushes on unstretched canvasses (tarpaulins, old printed tissues, etc.), and thereby inherited the function of restoring the full materiality of paint as such. For Pierre Buraglio, on the other hand, as for François Rouan, the important thing was first to *"produce surfaces upon which painting is possible"* (Buraglio). The former accomplished this by stressing the "picturality" of scrap material (assemblages of paper, coloured glass mounted on old window frames). The latter worked on the basis of patient weaving[1], in which paint reasserted its depth via the interlacing of fragments of abstract outlines and motifs.

Bernard Pagès also worked with assemblages, as did Patrick Saytour and Toni Grand; but these artists were more concerned with three-dimensional forms. By playing on the specific dynamism of natural, industrial or scrap materials, they made *"antagonistic pairings of forms working side by side"* (Pagès), *"uncomfortable attachments"* (Saytour), *"interventions"* and *"combinations"* (Toni Grand). All attempted to reveal the *"naturally opaque"* quality of Matter and the *"lasting instability"* of Form.

[1] From 1966 to 1980, the canvas was first tinted, then cut into strips, then rewoven. After 1980, this weaving process was "figured" with brushstroke hatching.

François Rouan
Volta faccia
Volte-face
1984
ink on paper on silk on cardboard 110 × 80

Claude Viallat
Fenêtre à Tahiti
Window in Tahiti
1976
acrylic and dye on an awning 207 × 170

Toni Grand
Bois flotté et stratifié, polyester et graphite
Stratified raft wood, polyester and graphite
1978
2 units: 21 × 328 × 22,5
and 17 × 330 × 23

1 Bernard Ceysson.

2 Catherine Francblin.

3 Maurice Besset.

In the mid-1970's, the renewal of representational art seemed the best recourse for a generation of painters seeking a way to assert their own individual sensibility, while at the same time becoming reconciled to the full heritage of art history. It was the "art of crisis," dictated by the *"search for a lost identity"*1 in a *"society adrift."*2

The *"Narrative Representation"* of the 1960's (Adami, Arroyo, Monory) had attempted to set up a critical iconography of contemporary life in terms of an ironical and decorative objectivity, conveyed in the detached style of photo-journalism. Their successors, the "Neo-Expressionist" representational art movements of the USA and Europe, did the opposite. They aimed for a kind of brutal telescoping of "high" and "low" cultural reminiscences, using personal symbols (Cucchi, Schnabel), primordial signs (Penck), historical myths (Kiefer), pictorial quotations (Garouste) or comic strip language (Blais, Combas, Di Rosa).

Paradoxically, this rebirth of representational art has a celebratory quality about it, though the celebration is an uneasy one. Its images are regarded as sacred, and yet brutalized; glorified, yet sullied by the aggression of the paintbrush; emptied of their original meaning (to the point of actual physical upending of canvasses, as in the work of the German painter Baselitz); or caught fragment by fragment and passionately and unself-consciously adopted *"... like a way of dressing."*3

It is as if painting were rubbed out, scraped, rinsed and emptied of everything except the debris from some distant shipwreck, vague evidence of something gone which would never return, and of a nostalgia which would remain forever.

But maybe the painter's art, relegated to the role of laughter in the dark and lamentation in the ruins, is up to another trick: maybe this period is a final masked ball before another resurrection.

Valerio Adami
Thorwaldsen
1980-81
acrylic on canvas 198 × 148

Georg Baselitz
Die mädchen von Olmo
The girls of Olmo
1981
oil on canvas 250 × 249

The winter garden
1968-70

In his Cycle *l'Hourloupe* (1962-73), Jean
Dubuffet sought to portray a *"continuous,
undifferentiated universe"* of physical reality
and mental representation. To achieve this,
he used a graphic system of abstract cellular
unities with improvised colours, which
resulted in a teeming puzzle, whose beginning
and end were completely arbitrary.
Dubuffet began by using this *"meandering,
uninterrupted and resolutely uniform
calligraphy,"*[1] which produced *"a liquefaction
of categories,"* to cover larger and larger
surfaces (1963-65). He went on to build
contorted *"simulacrums"* of ordinary objects
(1964-70), and finally, between 1969 and 1973,
to construct landscapes and edifices in resin
and epoxy that attained monumental
dimensions. The *Jardin d'Hiver* ("Winter
Garden") belongs to this last stage. It
represents *"a mental drift endowed with a
physical body,"* which jolts our customary
ideas about matter, distance and perspective;
and it *"sows doubt about the material reality
of the world we live in day by day."*[2] In this
way, Dubuffet contrives to suggest the
*"possibility, which remains open, that the
world could be recalculated and that thought
could be based on entirely different 'logos'."*[3]

[1] "Houle qui roule entourloupe
égale hourloupe"
Quoted by Max Loreau
Jean Dubuffet
Paris 1971

[2] Jean Dubuffet
Speech in New York
1972

[3] Jean Dubuffet
Letter to Arnold Glimcher
1969

Jean Dubuffet
Le jardin d'hiver
The winter garden
1968-70
painted resin
480 × 960 × 550

70

The Musée national d'art moderne permanent exhibitions

*may be viewed on the **3rd** and **4th floors** of the Pompidou Centre. They portray the evolution of Modern Art from 1905 to the present day in chronological order. Regular events are organised within this framework (see below).*
Opening hours: monday to friday 12 am - 10 pm
closed on tuesday
saturday and sunday 10 am - 10 pm

the temporary exhibition area
4th floor

is mainly devoted to work on paper (drawings, collages, aquarelles, engravings, photographs and illustrated books) exhibited in rotation.

the Museum cinema
3rd floor

gives regular showings of films from the Museum's documentary archives on Modern Art and artists.

the studio of the sculptor Brancusi

is on permanent exhibition on the piazza in front of the Pompidou Centre and laid out exactly as it was in its original home (Impasse Ronsin, in Paris). Brancusi willed his studio to the Museum on condition that it be displayed in this way.
*opening hours: call **42 77 12 33** ext. **4727***

temporary exhibitions at the Museum

These take place on various different floors of the Pompidou Centre:

on the 5th floor

many exhibitions are held each year in the Grand Galerie, on the major artists and artistic movements of the 20th century. These exhibitions cover many different forms of art and are often prepared in collaboration with the other departments of the Pompidou Centre.

on the ground floor
the Galeries Contemporaines

give priority to working artists from France and abroad, with a view to reflecting the full variety of today's artistic output.

in the forum

on the ground floor, the Museum mounts exhibitions of monumental works by contemporary artists, rotating with the Centre's other departments.

Constantin Brancusi
The artist's photography of his studio
c. 1935

services offered by the Musée national d'art moderne **71**

**the education section
of the Museum
offers**
*regular guided tours around the museum. These
tours are available to individuals carrying ordinary
museum entrance tickets, or to prearranged
groups; they cover both the permanent and the
temporary exhibitions organised by the Musée
national d'art moderne.*
for further information, call **42 77 12 33**, ext. **4625**
or **4673** 10 am to 1 pm
*modern art introductory courses, covering all the
main artistic movements of the 20th century.
training courses for teachers.*
for further information, call **42 77 12 33**, ext. **4625**
*conferences, debates and interviews enabling the
public to meet artists, art critics and writers
working on subjects related to the plastic arts.*
for further information, call **42 77 12 33**, ext. **4668**

**the Museum
documentation section**
*is located on the 2nd floor of the Pompidou
Centre, on the administrative side of the Museum.
Its purpose is to gather and preserve documents
relative to the plastic arts in the 20th century. The
documentation section has a reserve of 30 000
books (50% of which are freely available to the
public), 60 000 catalogues, 3 000 periodicals, 75 000
film transparencies (which can be viewed on the
premises), 20 000 files on artists, archives, etc.*
for further information, call **42 77 12 33**, ext. **4672**

edited by the Museum
*les Cahiers du Musée national d'art moderne: art
studies, exhibitions reports, essays by scholars.
catalogues raisonnés, guide-books, information
sheets, etc. concerning the collections of the
Museum.
catalogues, books, posters, slides, videotapes, etc.
concerning the temporary exhibitions of the
Museum.
All publications sold at the Museum's bookshop
(4th floor) and at the Centre's bookshop (ground-
floor).*
for further information, call **42 77 12 33**, ext. **4833**
or **4941**

Printed in Italy   March 1986
Photocomposition   l'Union Linotypiste
Photo-engraving   Scala

Design   Christophe Ibach
English layout   Gilbert Aichhorn
Translation   Anthony Roberts

Dépôt légal   3ᵉ trimestre 1986

Publisher number   504